# The Complete Renal Diet Cookbook for Beginners

Affordable, Quick & Easy Renal Recipes | Control Your Kidney Disease and Avoid Dialysis | 30-Day Meal Plan

Barben Bower

# Table of contents

# Introduction

Kidney disease, which has been dubbed as the "silent disease" for not having symptoms in the early stages, going undetected until it has progressed into very advanced stages, has always been a serious health concern in many parts of the world.

According to the National Kidney Foundation, up to 10 percent of the world's population suffers from chronic kidney disease. This condition is known to kill millions of people each year.

Kidney disease now ranks as the 18th deadliest condition in the world.

In the United States alone, it is reported that over 600,000 Americans succumb to kidney failure.

These stats are alarming, which is why, it is necessary to take proper care of your kidneys, starting with a kidney-friendly diet.

In this eBook, you will learn how to create dishes that are healthy, delicious and easy on your kidneys.

These recipes are ideal whether you have been diagnosed with a kidney problem or you want to prevent any kidney issue.

# Chapter 1: Kidney Disease and Diet

## Understanding Kidney Disease

Before we can go on to understand the disease that affects the kidneys, let us first get to know more about these two internal organs that play a significant role in the processes inside the body.

The kidneys are two internal organs that resemble the shape of a bean.
Each of these two kidneys is as the same size as your fist.
The main function of the kidneys is to filter out excess water as well as the wastes from your blood, and create urine.

Kidney disease occurs when your kidneys are not functioning the way they should.
Also called chronic kidney disease (CKD), this condition is characterized for the gradual loss of proper kidney function.

Once the disease reaches an advanced stage, the body suffers from dangerous buildup of fluid, wastes and electrolytes.

During the early stages, a person may show a few signs and symptoms. But it's also possible not to have any until the damage to the kidneys has become severe.

Treatment of this condition focuses primarily on slowing down the progression of the damage by taking control of the underlying causes. Without immediate treatment, it can immediately progress to advanced stage kidney failure, which can be life-threatening.

## What are the Causes of Kidney Disease?

Chronic kidney disease (CKD) is typically caused by another condition or disease that impairs proper functioning of the kidneys, causing progressive damage to these organs over time.

The most common health problems that because CKD include:

- Diabetes
- Hypertension
- Glomerulonephritis (inflammation or swelling of the glomeruli or the filtering units inside the kidneys)
- Interstitial nephritis (inflammation or swelling of the tubules in the kidneys or the structures surrounding these)

- Polycystic Kidney Disease (PKD)
- Obstruction inside the urinary tract due to kidney stones, certain types of cancer, enlarged prostate
- Vesicoureteral reflux (a medical condition that causes urine to go back to the kidneys)
- Pyelonephritis (a type of chronic kidney infection)

There are several factors that increase your risk of chronic kidney disease. These include the following:

- Diabetes
- High blood pressure
- Heart disease
- Disease in the blood vessels
- Smoking
- Obesity
- Race (African-American, Asian-American, Native American)
- Family history
- Abnormal kidney structure
- Old age

## Signs and Symptoms of Chronic Kidney Disease

As mentioned earlier, kidney disease is known as a "silent disease".

This is because most people who suffer from this condition do not become aware of it until the condition has reached advanced stage.

For those who experience signs and symptoms, these usually include the following:

- Nausea
- Vomiting
- Appetite loss
- Fatigue
- Weakness
- Difficulty sleeping
- Changes in urination
- Lack of focus
- Muscle cramps

- Muscle twitches
- Swelling of the feet and ankles
- Persistent skin itching
- Chest pains
- Shortness of breath
- High blood pressure.

It's important to know however that most of the signs and symptoms of kidney disease are nonspecific. This means that it's also possible that these symptoms are caused by other health problems.

You should also know that the kidneys are "highly adaptable", which means that they are able to compensate for damage or reduced function, which is why, you may not experience any of these symptoms until the damage has become so severe it can no longer be reversed or treated.

## Prevention of Kidney Disease

To reduce the risk of kidney disease, here are some preventive measures to keep in mind:

- Follow instructions when taking over-the-counter medications

Excessive intake of over-the-counter medications such as aspirin, ibuprofen (Motrin IB, Advil,) and acetaminophen (Tylenol) can cause damage in the kidneys. These medications should be avoided when you have already been diagnosed with kidney disease. It's imperative to consult your doctor first before taking any medications.

- Maintain an ideal weight

If you are overweight, it's imperative to engage in regular physical activity to start dropping pounds. Extra weight pressures the kidneys and makes them work harder when it comes to filtering wastes. Take note that a body mass index (BMI) 25 to 30 is considered overweight while BMI greater than 30 is referred to as obese.

- Do not smoke

Smoking can cause damage to your kidneys so it's advisable that you quit the nicotine habit before your kidneys take a hit.

- Manage and treat your medical conditions

Consult your doctor for the proper treatment of existing health problems such as diabetes and high blood pressure to prevent these from causing damage to your kidneys.

## What is Renal Diet?

One of the most effective ways to prevent kidney disease is with proper diet.

It's also important to know that those who are at risk of this disease or have already been diagnosed with this condition can help alleviate symptoms and slow down the progression of the disease with a diet called the renal diet.

As you know, the wastes in the blood come from the foods and drinks that you consume. When your kidneys are not functioning properly, they are unable to remove these wastes efficiently.

Wastes that remain in the blood can negatively affect your overall health.

Following a renal diet can help bolster the functioning of the kidney, reduce damage to the kidneys and prevent kidney failure.

So, what is a renal diet?

A renal diet is a type of diet that involves consumption of foods and drinks that are low in potassium, sodium and phosphorus.

It also puts focus on the consumption of high-quality protein as well as limiting too much intake of fluids and calcium.

Since each person's body is different, it's important to come up with a specific diet formulated by a dietician to make sure that the diet is tailored to the needs of the patient.

Some of the substances that you have to check and monitor for proper renal diet include:

## The Benefits of Renal Diet

A renal diet minimizes intake of sodium, potassium and phosphorus.

Excessive sodium is harmful to people who have been diagnosed with kidney disease as this causes fluid buildup, making it hard for the kidneys to eliminate sodium and fluid. Improper functioning of the kidneys can also mean difficulty in removing excess potassium.

When there is too much potassium in the body, this can lead to a condition called hyperkalemia, which can also cause problems with the heart and blood vessels. Kidneys that are not working efficiently find it difficult to remove excess phosphorus. High levels of phosphorus excrete calcium from the bones causing them to weaken. This also causes elevation of calcium deposits in the eyes, heart, lungs, and blood vessels.

## What to Eat and What to Avoid in Renal Diet

A renal diet focuses on foods that are natural and nutritious, but at the same time, are low in sodium, potassium and phosphorus.

Foods to eat:

- Cauliflower - 1 cup contains 19 mg sodium, 176 potassium, 40 mg phosphorus
- Blueberries - 1 cup contains 1.5 mg sodium, 114 potassium, 18 mg phosphorus
- Sea Bass - 3 ounces contain 74 mg sodium, 279 potassium, 211 mg phosphorus
- Grapes - 1/2 cup contains 1.5 mg sodium, 144 potassium, 15 mg phosphorus
- Egg Whites - 2 egg whites contain 110 mg sodium, 108 potassium, 10 mg phosphorus
- Garlic - 3 cloves contain 1.5 mg sodium, 36 potassium, 14 mg phosphorus
- Buckwheat - ½ cup contains 3.5 mg sodium, 74 potassium, 59 mg phosphorus
- Olive Oil - 1 ounce 0.6 mg sodium, 0.3 potassium, 0 mg phosphorus
- Bulgur - ½ cup contains 4.5 mg sodium, 62 potassium, 36 mg phosphorus
- Cabbage - 1 cup contains 13 mg sodium, 119 potassium, 18 mg phosphorus
- Skinless chicken - 3 ounces contain 63 mg sodium, 216 potassium, 192 mg phosphorus
- Bell peppers - 1 piece contains 3 mg sodium, 156 potassium, 19 mg phosphorus
- Onion - 1 piece contains 3 mg sodium, 102 potassium, 20 mg phosphorus
- Arugula - 1 cup contains 6 mg sodium, 74 potassium, 10 mg phosphorus
- Macadamia nuts - 1 ounce contains 1.4 mg sodium, 103 potassium, 53 mg phosphorus
- Radish - ½ cup contains 23 mg sodium, 135 potassium, 12 mg phosphorus
- Turnips - ½ cup contains 12.5 mg sodium, 138 potassium, 20 mg phosphorus
- Pineapple - 1 cup contains 2 mg sodium, 180 potassium, 13 mg phosphorus
- Cranberries – 1 cup contains 2 mg sodium, 85 potassium, 13 mg phosphorus
- Mushrooms – 1 cup contains 6 mg sodium, 170 potassium, 42 mg phosphorus

Foods to Avoid:

These foods are known to have high levels of potassium, sodium or phosphorus:

- Soda – Soda is believed to contain up to 100 mg of additive phosphorus per 200 ml.
- Avocados - 1 cup contains up to 727 mg of potassium.
- Canned foods – Canned foods contain high amounts of sodium so make sure that you avoid using these, or at least, opt for low-sodium versions.
- Whole wheat bread – 1 ounce of bread contains 57 mg phosphorus and 69 mg potassium, which is higher compared to white bread.
- Brown rice – 1 cup of brown rice contains 154 mg potassium while 1 cup of white rice only has 54 mg potassium.
- Bananas – 1 banana contains 422 mg potassium.
- Dairy – Dairy products is high in potassium, phosphorus and calcium. You can still consume dairy products but you have to limit it. Use dairy milk alternatives like almond milk and coconut milk.
- Processed Meats – Processed meats are not advisable to people with kidney problems because of their high content of additives and preservatives.
- Pickled and cured foods – These are made using large amounts of salt.
- Apricots – 1 cup contains 427 mg potassium.
- Potatoes and sweet potatoes – 1 potato contain 610 mg potassium. You can double boil potatoes and sweet potatoes to reduce potassium by 50 percent.
- Tomatoes – 1 cup tomato sauce contains up to 900 mg potassium.
- Instant meals – Instant meals are known for extremely high amounts of sodium.
- Spinach – Spinach contains up to 290 mg potassium per cup. Cooking helps reduce the amount of potassium.
- Raisins, prunes and dates – Dried fruits have concentrated nutrients including potassium. 1 cup prunes contain up to 1,274 mg potassium.
- Chips – Chips are known to have high amounts of sodium.

# Chapter 2: 30-Day Meal Plan

Day 1

Breakfast: Apple and Cinnamon French Toast

Lunch: Fish with Mushrooms

Dinner: Tofu Stir Fry

Day 2

Breakfast: Sour Cream Pancakes

Lunch: Basil Chicken

Dinner: Dijon Pork Chops

Day 3

Breakfast: Oatmeal with Fruits

Lunch: Herbed Pork Chops

Dinner: Seasoned Green Beans

Day 4

Breakfast: Breakfast Trail Mix

Lunch: Barbecue Beef

Dinner: Baked Trout

Day 5

Breakfast: Plain Pancakes with Almond Milk

Lunch: Turkey Meatloaf

Dinner: Eggplant Fries

Day 6

Breakfast: Corn and Zucchini Omelet

Lunch: Pork Souvlaki

Dinner: Grilled Squash

Day 7

Breakfast: Breakfast Casserole

Lunch: Fish Taco

Dinner: Vegetable Medley

Day 8

Breakfast: Apple and Cinnamon French Toast

Lunch: Basil Chicken

Dinner: Lemon Butter Salmon

Day 9

Breakfast: Italian Eggs with Peppers

Lunch: Roasted Lamb

Dinner: Turkey with Curry Glaze

Day 10

Breakfast: Strawberry Breakfast Smoothie

Lunch: Barbecue Beef

Dinner: Cauliflower Rice

Day 11

Breakfast: Bulgur with Coconut Milk

Lunch: Italian Beef

Dinner: Herbed Pork Chops

Day 12

Breakfast: Double Boiled Potato Hash

Lunch: Zesty Chicken

Dinner: Shrimp in Garlic Sauce

Day 13

Breakfast: Oatmeal with Apple Slices

Lunch: Balsamic Pork Chops

Dinner: Shrimp and Broccoli

Day 14

Breakfast: Dill Scrambled Eggs

Lunch: Carrot Casserole

Dinner: Crispy Lemon Chicken

Day 15

Breakfast: Blueberry Smoothie in A Bowl

Lunch: Beef and Broccoli

Dinner: Broccoli Pancake

Day 16

Breakfast: Breakfast Trail Mix

Lunch: Shish Kebabs

Dinner: Rosemary Chicken with Veggies

Day 17

Breakfast: Acai Berry Smoothie Bowl

Lunch: Vegetable Medley

Dinner: Baked Fish in Cream Sauce

Day 18

Breakfast: Sweet Potatoes (Double Boiled)

Lunch: Turkey Meatloaf

Dinner: Braised Beef

Day 19

Breakfast: Corn and Zucchini Omelet

Lunch: Shrimp and Broccoli

Dinner: Tofu Stir Fry

Day 20

Breakfast: Double Boiled Potato Hash

Lunch: Pork Souvlaki

Dinner: Sweet and Sour Chicken

Day 21

Breakfast: Blueberry Smoothie in A Bowl

Lunch: Crab Cake

Dinner: Turkey Meatloaf

Day 22

Breakfast: Egg Pockets

Lunch: Balsamic Pork Chops

Dinner: Grilled Squash

Day 23

Breakfast: Italian Eggs with Peppers

Lunch: Tofu Stir Fry

Dinner: Chicken Marsala

Day 24

Breakfast: Sweet Potatoes (Double Boiled)

Lunch: Braised Beef

Dinner: Shrimp in Garlic Sauce

Day 25

Breakfast: Acai Berry Smoothie Bowl

Lunch: Lemon Butter Salmon

Dinner: Zesty Chicken

Day 26

Breakfast: Mushroom Omelet

Lunch: Baked Fish in Cream Sauce

Dinner: Baked Pork Chops

Day 27

Breakfast: Breakfast Casserole

Lunch: Baked Pork Chops

Dinner: Crispy Lemon Chicken

Day 28

Breakfast: Mushroom Omelet

Lunch: Seasoned Green Beans

Dinner: Shrimp and Broccoli

Day 29

Breakfast: Egg Pockets

Lunch: Broccoli Pancake

Dinner: Baked Trout

Day 30

Breakfast: Sour Cream Pancakes

Lunch: Lemon Butter Salmon

Dinner: Zesty Chicken

# Chapter 3: Breakfast

## Sour Cream Pancakes

Preparation Time: 10 minutes
Cooking Time: 10 minutes
Servings: 4

Ingredients:

- 2 eggs, beaten
- 1/2 cup cottage cheese
- 1/2 cup sour cream
- Salt to taste
- 1/2 cup all-purpose flour

Method:

1. Mix all ingredients except flour in a blender.
2. Fold in the flour.
3. Cook batter in a skillet over medium heat.
4. Flip when the surface starts to bubble.
5. Cook until firm.

Nutritional Value:

- Calories 165
- Protein 8 g
- Carbohydrates 13 g
- Fat 9 g
- Cholesterol 123 mg
- Sodium 150 mg
- Potassium 111 mg
- Phosphorus 134 mg
- Calcium 64 mg
- Fiber 0.4 g

# Apple & Cinnamon French Toast

Preparation Time: 20 minutes
Cooking Time: 50 minutes
Servings: 12

Ingredients:

- Cooking spray
- 1 lb. loaf cinnamon raisin bread, cubed
- 8 oz. cream cheese, cubed
- 1 apple, diced
- 6 tablespoons butter
- 1 teaspoon ground cinnamon
- 8 eggs
- 1 cup half and half
- ¼ cup pancake syrup
- 1 cup almond milk

Method:

1. Spray oil on a baking dish.
2. Arrange half of the bread cubes and sprinkle cream cheese on top.
3. Top with the apples.
4. Sprinkle the cinnamon over the apple and bread.
5. Top with the remaining bread cubes.
6. In a bowl, beat eggs with half and half.
7. Add syrup, almond milk and butter.
8. Pour mixture over the bread.
9. Cover with foil.
10. Refrigerate for 2 hours.
11. Bake in the oven at 325 degrees F for 50 minutes.
12. Let cool for 10 minutes before serving.
13. Slice into 12 servings.

Nutritional Value:

- Calories 324
- Protein 9 g

- Carbohydrates 27 g
- Fat 20 g
- Cholesterol 170 mg
- Sodium 280 mg
- Potassium 224 mg
- Phosphorus 150 mg
- Fiber 1.8 g

# Blueberry Smoothie in a Bowl

Preparation Time: 15 minutes
Cooking Time: 0 minutes
Serving: 1

Ingredients:

- 1 cup frozen blueberries
- 1/4 cup plain Greek yogurt
- 2 tablespoons whey protein powder
- 1/4 cup vanilla almond milk (unsweetened)
- 1 tablespoon cereal
- 5 raspberries, sliced
- 2 strawberries, sliced
- 2 teaspoons coconut flakes

Method:

1. Put the blueberries, yogurt, whey protein powder and almond milk in a blender.
2. Blend until smooth.
3. Pour mixture into a bowl.
4. Top with cereal, raspberries and strawberries.
5. Sprinkle coconut flakes on top.

Nutritional Value:

- Calories 225
- Protein 17 g
- Carbohydrates 28 g
- Fat 5 g
- Cholesterol 3 mg
- Sodium 118 mg
- Potassium 370 mg
- Phosphorus 174 mg
- Calcium 240 mg
- Fiber 7.8 g

# Breakfast Casserole

Preparation Time: 15 minutes
Cooking Time: 55 minutes
Servings: 9

Ingredients:

- 8 oz. low fat sausage, crumbled
- 8 oz. cream cheese
- 1 cup almond milk
- 4 slices white bread, cut into cubes
- 5 eggs
- 1/2 teaspoon dry mustard
- 1/2 teaspoon dried onion flakes

Method:

1. Preheat your oven to 325 degrees F.
2. In a skillet, cook sausage in medium heat and then set aside.
3. In a blender, put the rest of the ingredients except the bread.
4. Pulse until well blended.
5. Pour mixture into a bowl.
6. Add the sausage.
7. Add mixture to a casserole dish.
8. Bake for 55 minutes.

Nutritional Value:

- Calories 224
- Protein 11 g
- Carbohydrates 9 g
- Fat 16 g
- Cholesterol 149 mg
- Sodium 356 mg
- Potassium 201 mg
- Phosphorus 159 mg
- Calcium 97 mg
- Fiber 0.4 g

# Egg Pockets

Preparation Time: 15 minutes
Cooking Time: 20 minutes
Servings: 4

Ingredients:

- 1 teaspoon dry yeast
- 1 cup warm water
- 1 tablespoon oil
- 1 teaspoon garlic powder
- 2 cups all-purpose flour
- 1 tablespoon sugar
- 3 eggs, beat
- Cooking spray

Method:

1. Dissolve the yeast in water.
2. Add the oil, garlic powder, flour and sugar.
3. Form soft dough from the mixture.
4. Let it sit for 5 minutes.
5. Roll out the dough and slice into 4 portions.
6. Create a bowl with the dough.
7. Beat the eggs.
8. Put egg on top of the dough.
9. Fold the dough and pinch the edges.
10. Bake in the oven at 350 degrees F for 20 minutes.

Nutritional Value:

- Calories 321
- Protein 11 g
- Carbohydrates 25 g
- Fat 7 g
- Cholesterol 123 mg
- Sodium 50 mg
- Potassium 139 mg
- Phosphorus 130 mg
- Calcium 30 mg

- Fiber 2 g

# Italian Eggs with Peppers

Preparation Time: 15 minutes
Cooking Time: 20 minutes
Servings: 6

Ingredients:

- 1/2 cup onion, minced
- 1 cup red bell pepper, chopped
- 8 eggs, beaten
- Black pepper to taste
- 1/4 cup fresh basil, chopped

Method:

1. In a skillet, cook onion and red bell pepper until soft.
2. Season eggs with black pepper.
3. Pour egg mixture into the pan.
4. Cook without mixing until firm.
5. Sprinkle fresh basil on top before serving.

Nutritional Value:

- Calories 194
- Protein 13 g
- Carbohydrates 5 g
- Fat 14 g
- Cholesterol 423 mg
- Sodium 141 mg
- Potassium 222 mg
- Phosphorus 203 mg
- Calcium 64 mg
- Fiber 0.8 g

# Mushroom Omelet

Preparation Time: 10 minutes
Cooking Time: 5 minutes
Servings: 2

Ingredients:

- 2 teaspoons butter
- 2 tablespoons onion, chopped
- 1/2 cup mushroom, diced
- 1/4 cup sweet red peppers, chopped
- 3 eggs, beaten
- 1 teaspoon Worcestershire sauce
- 1/4 teaspoon black pepper

Method:

1. Melt butter in a pan over medium heat.
2. Cook the onion, mushroom and sweet peppers for 5 minutes.
3. Remove from the pan and set aside.
4. Mix the eggs and Worcestershire sauce.
5. Cook eggs over medium heat.
6. When the edges start to become firm, add onion mixture on top.
7. Season with pepper.
8. Fold the omelet.

Nutritional Value:

- Calories 199
- Protein 11 g
- Carbohydrates 4 g
- Fat 15 g
- Cholesterol 341 mg
- Sodium 276 mg
- Potassium 228 mg
- Phosphorus 167 mg
- Calcium 55 mg
- Fiber 0.6 g

# Corn & Zucchini Omelet

Preparation Time: 15 minutes
Cooking Time: 5 minutes
Serving: 1

Ingredients:

- Cooking spray
- 3 tablespoons green onion, chopped
- 1/4 cup corn kernels, thawed
- 1/3 cup zucchini, chopped
- 2 tablespoons water
- 1/4 teaspoon herb seasoning blend
- 2 egg whites
- 1 egg
- 1 oz. cheddar cheese, shredded

Method:

1. Spray pan with oil.
2. Cook onion, corn and zucchini for 4 minutes.
3. Remove from the stove and set aside.
4. In a bowl, mix the egg, egg whites, water and pepper.
5. Pour mixture into the pan and cook for 2 minutes.
6. Put the onion mixture on top of the egg.
7. Sprinkle cheese on top.
8. Fold into an omelet.

Nutritional Value:

- Calories 187
- Protein 22 g
- Carbohydrates 12 g
- Fat 6 g
- Cholesterol 215 mg
- Sodium 270 mg
- Potassium 352 mg
- Phosphorus 218 mg
- Calcium 165 mg
- Fiber 2.2 g

# Breakfast Trail Mix

Preparation Time: 15 minutes
Cooking Time: 25 minutes
Servings: 24

Ingredients:

- 3 cups cereal
- 5 cups rice cereal
- 10 oz. graham cookies
- 6 oz. pretzel chips
- 1/2 cup butter
- 1/4 cup brown sugar
- 1/4 cup maple syrup
- 1/4 cup honey
- 3 oz. apple chips
- 5 oz. dried unsweetened cranberries

Method:

1. Put the cereal, rice cereal, graham cookies and pretzel chips in a bowl.
2. Toss to mix.
3. In a saucepan over low heat, melt the butter.
4. Stir in the sugar, maple syrup and honey.
5. Cook until the sugar is dissolved.
6. Pour mixture over the cereals.
7. Mix well.
8. Arrange in a baking pan.
9. Bake at 325 degrees F for 20 minutes.
10. Add the apple chips and cranberries on top.
11. Bake for another 5 minutes.

Nutritional Value:

- Calories 262
- Protein 3 g
- Carbohydrates 47 g
- Fat 9 g

- Cholesterol 11 mg
- Sodium 178 mg
- Potassium 84 mg
- Phosphorus 66 mg
- Calcium 63 mg
- Fiber 1.8 g

# Acai Berry Smoothie Bowl

Preparation Time: 10 minutes
Cooking Time: 0 minutes
Servings: 2

Ingredients:

- 1 cup acai berry
- 1 cup frozen berries
- ¾ cup low fat Greek yogurt
- 1 teaspoon chia seeds
- 1/2 cup rice milk (unsweetened)
- 2 tablespoons blueberries, sliced
- 2 tablespoons raspberries, sliced
- 1/4 fresh pear, sliced

Method:

1. Put all the ingredients except blueberries, raspberries and pear in a blender.
2. Blend until smooth.
3. Pour mixture into a bowl.
4. Top with the sliced fruits.

Nutritional Value:

- Calories 192
- Protein 11 g
- Carbohydrates 28 g
- Fat 4 g
- Cholesterol 0 mg
- Sodium 82 mg
- Potassium 349 mg
- Phosphorus 140 mg
- Calcium 298 mg
- Fiber 7.2 g

# Chapter 4: Soups and Stews

## Chicken Noodle Soup

Preparation Time: 15 minutes
Cooking Time: 25 minutes
Servings: 4

Ingredients:

- 1 cup low-sodium chicken broth
- 1 cup water
- 1/4 teaspoon poultry seasoning
- 1/4 teaspoon black pepper
- 1/4 cup carrot, chopped
- 1 cup chicken, cooked and shredded
- 2 ounces egg noodles

Method:

1. Add broth and water in a slow cooker.
2. Set the pot to high.
3. Add poultry seasoning and pepper.
4. Add carrot, chicken and egg noodles to the pot.
5. Cook on high setting for 25 minutes.
6. Serve while warm.

Nutritional Value:

- Calories 141
- Protein 15 g
- Carbohydrates 11 g
- Fat 4 g
- Cholesterol 49 mg
- Sodium 191 mg
- Potassium 135 mg
- Phosphorus 104 mg
- Calcium 16 mg
- Fiber 0.7 g

# Beef Stew with Apple Cider

Preparation Time: 15 minutes
Cooking Time: 10 hours
Servings: 8

Ingredients:

- 1/2 cup potatoes, cubed
- 2 lb. beef cubes
- 7 tablespoons all-purpose flour, divided
- 1/4 teaspoon thyme
- Black pepper to taste
- 3 tablespoons oil
- ¼ cup carrot, sliced
- 1 cup onion, diced
- 1/2 cup celery, diced
- 1 cup apples, diced
- 2 cups apple cider
- 1/2 cups water
- 2 tablespoons apple cider vinegar

Method:

1. Double boil the potatoes (to reduce the amount of potassium) in a pot of water.
2. In a shallow dish, mix the half of the flour, thyme and pepper.
3. Coat all sides of beef cubes with the mixture.
4. In a pan over medium heat, add the oil and cook the beef cubes until brown. Set aside.
5. Layer the ingredients in your slow cooker.
6. Put the carrots, potatoes, onions, celery, beef and apple.
7. In a bowl, mix the cider, vinegar and 1 cup water.
8. Add this to the slow cooker.
9. Cook on low setting for 10 hours.
10. Stir in the remaining flour to thicken the soup.

Nutritional Value:

- Calories 365

- Protein 33 g
- Carbohydrates 20 g
- Fat 17 g
- Cholesterol 73 mg
- Sodium 80 mg
- Potassium 540 mg
- Phosphorus 234 mg
- Calcium 36 mg
- Fiber 2.2 g

# Chicken Chili

Preparation Time: 20 minutes
Cooking Time: 1 hour and 15 minutes
Servings: 8

Ingredients:

- 1 tablespoon oil
- 1 cup onion, chopped
- 4 garlic cloves, chopped
- 1 cup green pepper
- 1 cup celery, chopped
- 1 cup carrots, chopped
- 14 oz. low-sodium chicken broth
- 1 lb. chicken breast, cubed and cooked
- 1 cup low-sodium tomatoes, drained and iced
- 1 cup kidney beans, rinsed and drained
- 3/4 cup salsa
- 3 tablespoons chili powder
- 1 teaspoon ground oregano
- 4 cups white rice, cooked

Method:

1. In a pot, pour oil and cook onion, garlic, green pepper, celery and carrots.
2. Add the broth.
3. Bring to a boil.
4. Add the rest of the ingredients except the rice.
5. Simmer for 1 hour.
6. Serve with rice.

Nutritional Value:

- Calories 355
- Protein 24 g
- Carbohydrates 38 g
- Fat 12 g
- Cholesterol 59 mg

- Sodium 348 mg
- Potassium 653 mg
- Phosphorus 270 mg
- Calcium 133 mg
- Fiber 4.7 g

# Lamb Stew

Preparation Time: 30 minutes
Cooking Time: 1 hour and 40 minutes
Servings: 6

Ingredients:

- 1 lb. boneless lamb shoulder, trimmed and cubes
- Black pepper to taste
- 1/4 cup all-purpose flour
- 1 tablespoon olive oil
- 1 onion, chopped
- 3 garlic cloves, chopped
- 1/2 cup tomato sauce
- 2 cups low-sodium beef broth
- 1 teaspoon dried thyme
- 2 parsnips, sliced
- 2 carrots, sliced
- 1 cup frozen peas

Method:

1. Season lamb with pepper.
2. Coat evenly with flour.
3. Pour oil in a pot over medium heat.
4. Cook the lamb and then set aside.
5. Add onion to the pot.
6. Cook for 2 minutes.
7. Add garlic and saute for 30 seconds.
8. Pour in the broth to deglaze the pot.
9. Add the tomato sauce and thyme.
10. Put the lamb back to the pot.
11. Bring to a boil and then simmer for 1 hour.
12. Add parsnips and carrots.
13. Cook for 30 minutes.
14. Add green peas and cook for 5 minutes.

Nutritional Value:

- Calories 283
- Protein 27 g
- Carbohydrates 19 g
- Fat 11 g
- Cholesterol 80 mg
- Sodium 325 mg
- Potassium 527 mg
- Phosphorus 300 mg
- Calcium 56 mg
- Fiber 3.4 g

# Sausage & Egg Soup

Preparation Time: 15 minutes
Cooking Time: 30 minutes
Servings: 4

Ingredients:

- 1/2 lb. ground beef
- Black pepper
- 1/2 teaspoon ground sage
- 1/2 teaspoon garlic powder
- 1/2 teaspoon dried basil
- 4 slices bread (one day old), cubed
- 2 tablespoons olive oil
- 1 tablespoon herb seasoning blend
- 2 garlic cloves, minced
- 3 cups low-sodium chicken broth
- 1 cup water
- 4 tablespoons fresh parsley
- 4 eggs
- 2 tablespoons Parmesan cheese, grated

Method:

1. Preheat your oven to 375 degrees F.
2. Mix the first five ingredients to make the sausage.
3. Toss bread cubes in oil and seasoning blend.
4. Bake in the oven for 8 minutes. Set aside.
5. Cook the sausage in a pan over medium heat.
6. Cook the garlic in the sausage drippings for 2 minutes.
7. Stir in the broth, water and parsley.
8. Bring to a boil and then simmer for 10 minutes.
9. Pour into serving bowls and top with baked bread, egg and sausage.

Nutritional Value:

- Calories 335
- Protein 26 g

- Carbohydrates 15 g
- Fat 19 g
- Cholesterol 250 mg
- Sodium 374 mg
- Potassium 392 mg
- Phosphorus 268 mg
- Calcium 118 mg
- Fiber 0.9 g

# Spring Veggie Soup

Preparation Time: 20 minutes
Cooking Time: 45 minutes
Servings: 5

Ingredients:

- 2 tablespoons olive oil
- 1/2 cup onion, diced
- 1/2 cup mushrooms, sliced
- 1/8 cup celery, chopped
- 1 tomato, diced
- 1/2 cup carrots, diced
- 1 cup green beans, trimmed
- 1/2 cup frozen corn
- 1 teaspoon garlic powder
- 1 teaspoon dried oregano leaves
- 4 cups low-sodium vegetable broth

Method:

1. In a pot, pour the olive oil and cook the onion and celery for 2 minutes.
2. Add the rest of the ingredients.
3. Bring to a boil.
4. Reduce heat and simmer for 45 minutes.

Nutritional Value:

- Calories 114
- Protein 2 g
- Carbohydrates 13 g
- Fat 6 g
- Cholesterol 0 mg
- Sodium 262 mg
- Potassium 400 mg
- Phosphorus 108 mg
- Calcium 48 mg
- Fiber 3.4 g

# Seafood Chowder with Corn

Preparation Time: 15 minutes
Cooking Time: 20 minutes
Servings: 10

Ingredients:

- 1 tablespoon butter (unsalted)
- 1 cup onion, chopped
- 1/2 cup red bell pepper, chopped
- 1/2 cup green bell pepper, chopped
- 1/4 cup celery, chopped
- 1 tablespoon all-purpose white flour
- 14 oz. low-sodium chicken broth
- 2 cups non-dairy creamer
- 6 oz. almond milk
- 10 oz. crab flakes
- 2 cups corn kernels
- 1/2 teaspoon paprika
- Black pepper to taste

Method:

1. In a pan over medium heat, melt the butter and cook the onion, bell peppers and celery for 4 minutes.
2. Stir in the flour and cook for 2 minutes.
3. Add the broth and bring to a boil.
4. Add the rest of the ingredients.
5. Stir occasionally, and cook for 5 minutes.

Nutritional Value:

- Calories 173
- Protein 8 g
- Carbohydrates 22 g
- Fat 7 g
- Cholesterol 13 mg
- Sodium 160 mg
- Potassium 285 mg
- Phosphorus 181 mg
- Calcium 68 mg
- Fiber 1.5 g

# Taco Soup

Preparation Time: 30 minutes
Cooking Time: 7 hours
Servings: 10

Ingredients:

- 1 lb. chicken breast (boneless, skinless)
- 15 oz. canned red kidney beans, rinsed and drained
- 15 oz. low-sodium white corn, rinsed and drained
- 15 oz. canned yellow hominy, rinsed and drained
- 1 cup canned diced tomatoes with green chilies
- 1/2 cup onion, chopped
- 1/2 cup green bell peppers, chopped
- 1 clove garlic, chopped
- 1 jalapeno, chopped
- 1 tablespoon low-sodium taco seasoning
- 2 cups low-sodium chicken broth

Method:

1. Put chicken in the slow cooker.
2. Top with the rest of the ingredients.
3. Cook on high for 1 hour.
4. Set to low and cook for 6 hours.
5. Shred chicken and serve with the soup.

Nutritional Value:

- Calories 190
- Protein 21 g
- Carbohydrates 19 g
- Fat 3 g
- Cholesterol 42 mg
- Sodium 421 mg
- Potassium 444 mg
- Phosphorus 210 mg
- Calcium 28 mg
- Fiber 4.3 g

# Chapter 5: Fish and Seafood

## Lemon Butter Salmon

Preparation Time: 15 minutes
Cooking Time: 15 minutes
Servings: 6

Ingredients:

- 1 tablespoon butter
- 2 tablespoons olive oil
- 1 tablespoon Dijon mustard
- 1 tablespoons lemon juice
- 2 cloves garlic, crushed
- 1 teaspoon dried dill
- 1 teaspoon dried basil leaves
- 1 tablespoon capers
- 24 oz. salmon filet

Method:

1. Put all the ingredients except the salmon in a saucepan over medium heat.
2. Bring to a boil and then simmer for 5 minutes.
3. Preheat your grill.
4. Create a packet using foil.
5. Place the sauce and salmon inside.
6. Seal the packet.
7. Grill for 12 minutes.

Nutritional Value:

- Calories 294
- Protein 23 g
- Carbohydrates 1 g
- Fat 22 g
- Cholesterol 68 mg
- Sodium 190 mg
- Potassium 439 mg
- Phosphorus 280 mg
- Calcium 21 mg

# Crab Cake

Preparation Time: 15 minutes
Cooking Time: 9 minutes
Servings: 6

Ingredients:

- 1/4 cup onion, chopped
- 1/4 cup bell pepper, chopped
- 1 egg, beaten
- 6 low-sodium crackers, crushed
- 1/4 cup low-fat mayonnaise
- 1 lb. crab meat
- 1 tablespoon dry mustard
- Pepper to taste
- 2 tablespoons lemon juice
- 1 tablespoon fresh parsley
- 1 tablespoon garlic powder
- 3 tablespoons olive oil

Method:

1. Mix all the ingredients except the oil.
2. Form 6 patties from the mixture.
3. Pour the oil into a pan over medium heat.
4. Cook the crab cakes for 5 minutes.
5. Flip and cook for another 4 minutes.

Nutritional Value:

- Calories 188
- Protein 13 g
- Carbohydrates 5 g
- Fat 13 g
- Cholesterol 111 mg
- Sodium 342 mg
- Potassium 317 mg
- Phosphorus 185 mg
- Calcium 52 mg
- Fiber 0.5 g

# Baked Fish in Cream Sauce

Preparation Time: 10 minutes
Cooking Time: 40 minutes
Servings: 4

Ingredients:

- 1 lb. haddock
- 1/2 cup all-purpose flour
- 2 tablespoons butter (unsalted)
- 1/4 teaspoon pepper
- 2 cups fat-free nondairy creamer
- 1/4 cup water

Method:

1. Preheat your oven to 350 degrees F.
2. Spray baking pan with oil.
3. Sprinkle with a little flour.
4. Arrange fish on the pan
5. Season with pepper.
6. Sprinkle remaining flour on the fish.
7. Spread creamer on both sides of the fish.
8. Bake for 40 minutes or until golden.
9. Spread cream sauce on top of the fish before serving.

Nutritional Value:

- Calories 380
- Protein 23 g
- Carbohydrates 46 g
- Fat 11 g
- Cholesterol 79 mg
- Sodium 253 mg
- Potassium 400 mg
- Phosphorus 266 mg
- Calcium 46 mg
- Fiber 0.4 g

# Shrimp & Broccoli

Preparation Time: 10 minutes
Cooking Time: 5 minutes
Servings: 4

Ingredients:

- 1 tablespoon olive oil
- 1 clove garlic, minced
- 1 lb. shrimp
- 1/4 cup red bell pepper
- 1 cup broccoli florets, steamed
- 10 oz. cream cheese
- 1/2 teaspoon garlic powder
- 1/4 cup lemon juice
- 3/4 teaspoon ground peppercorns
- 1/4 cup half and half creamer

Method:

1. In a pan over medium heat, pour the oil and cook garlic for 30 seconds.
2. Add shrimp and cook for 2 minutes.
3. Add the rest of the ingredients.
4. Mix well.
5. Cook for 2 minutes.

Nutritional Value:

- Calories 468
- Protein 27 g
- Carbohydrates 28 g
- Fat 28 g
- Cholesterol 213 mg
- Sodium 374 mg
- Potassium 469 mg
- Phosphorus 335 mg
- Calcium 157 mg
- Fiber 2.6 g

# Shrimp in Garlic Sauce

Preparation Time: 10 minutes
Cooking Time: 6 minutes
Servings: 4

Ingredients:

- 3 tablespoons butter (unsalted)
- 1/4 cup onion, minced
- 3 cloves garlic, minced
- 1 lb. shrimp, shelled and deveined
- 1/2 cup half and half creamer
- 1/4 cup white wine
- 2 tablespoons fresh basil
- Black pepper to taste

Method:

1. Add butter to a pan over medium low heat.
2. Let it melt.
3. Add the onion and garlic.
4. Cook for 1 minute.
5. Add the shrimp and cook for 2 minutes.
6. Transfer shrimp on a serving platter and set aside.
7. Add the rest of the ingredients.
8. Simmer for 3 minutes.
9. Pour sauce over the shrimp and serve.

Nutritional Value:

- Calories 483
- Protein 32 g
- Carbohydrates 46 g
- Fat 19 g
- Cholesterol 230 mg
- Sodium 213 mg
- Potassium 514 mg
- Phosphorus 398 mg
- Calcium 133 mg
- Fiber 2.0 g

# Fish Taco

Preparation Time: 40 minutes
Cooking Time: 10 minutes
Servings: 6

Ingredients:

- 1 tablespoon lime juice
- 1 tablespoon olive oil
- 1 clove garlic, minced
- 1 lb. cod fillets
- 1/2 teaspoon ground cumin
- 1/4 teaspoon black pepper
- 1/2 teaspoon chili powder
- 1/4 cup sour cream
- 1/2 cup mayonnaise
- 2 tablespoons nondairy milk
- 1 cup cabbage, shredded
- 1/2 cup onion, chopped
- 1/2 bunch cilantro, chopped
- 12 corn tortillas

Method:

1. Drizzle lemon juice over the fish fillet.
2. Coat with olive oil and season with garlic, cumin, pepper and chili powder.
3. Let it sit for 30 minutes.
4. Broil fish for 10 minutes, flipping halfway through.
5. Flake the fish using a fork.
6. In a bowl, mix sour cream, milk and mayo.
7. Assemble tacos by filling each tortilla with mayo mixture, cabbage, onion, cilantro and fish flakes.

Nutritional Value:

- Calories 363
- Protein 18 g
- Carbohydrates 30 g

- Fat 19 g
- Cholesterol 40 mg
- Sodium 194 mg
- Potassium 507 mg
- Phosphorus 327 mg
- Calcium 138 mg
- Fiber 4.3 g

# Baked Trout

Preparation Time: 5 minutes
Cooking Time: 10 minutes
Servings: 8

Ingredients:

- 2 lb. trout fillet
- 1 tablespoon oil
- 1 teaspoon salt-free lemon pepper
- 1/2 teaspoon paprika

Method:

1. Preheat your oven to 350 degrees F.
2. Coat fillet with oil.
3. Place fish on a baking pan.
4. Season with lemon pepper and paprika.
5. Bake for 10 minutes.

Nutritional Value:

- Calories 161
- Protein 21 g
- Carbohydrates 0 g
- Fat 8 g
- Cholesterol 58 mg
- Sodium 109 mg
- Potassium 385 mg
- Phosphorus 227 mg
- Calcium 75 mg
- Fiber 0.1 g

# Fish with Mushrooms

Preparation Time: 5 minutes
Cooking Time: 16 minutes
Servings: 4

Ingredients:

- 1 lb. cod fillet
- 2 tablespoons butter
- ¼ cup white onion, chopped
- 1 cup fresh mushrooms
- 1 teaspoon dried thyme

Method:

1. Put the fish in a baking pan.
2. Preheat your oven to 450 degrees F.
3. In a pan over medium heat, melt the butter and cook onion and mushroom for 1 minute.
4. Spread mushroom mixture on top of the fish.
5. Season with thyme.
6. Bake in the oven for 15 minutes.

Nutritional Value:

- Calories 155
- Protein 21 g
- Carbohydrates 2 g
- Fat 7 g
- Cholesterol 49 mg
- Sodium 110 mg
- Potassium 561 mg
- Phosphorus 225 mg
- Calcium 30 mg
- Fiber 0.5 g

# Chapter 6: Vegetarian

## Tofu Stir Fry

Preparation Time: 15 minutes
Cooking Time: 20 minutes
Servings: 4

Ingredients:

- 1 teaspoon sugar
- 1 tablespoon lime juice
- 1 tablespoon low sodium soy sauce
- 2 tablespoons cornstarch
- 2 egg whites, beaten
- 1/2 cup unseasoned bread crumbs
- 1 tablespoon vegetable oil
- 16 ounces tofu, cubed
- 1 clove garlic, minced
- 1 tablespoon sesame oil
- 1 red bell pepper, sliced into strips
- 1 cup broccoli florets
- 1 teaspoon herb seasoning blend
- Dash black pepper
- Sesame seeds
- Steamed white rice

Method:

1. Dissolve sugar in a mixture of lime juice and soy sauce. Set aside.
2. In the first bowl, put the cornstarch.
3. Add the egg whites in the second bowl.
4. Place the breadcrumbs in the third bowl.
5. Dip each tofu cubes in the first, second and third bowls.
6. Pour vegetable oil in a pan over medium heat.
7. Cook tofu cubes until golden.
8. Drain the tofu and set aside.
9. Remove oil from the pan and add sesame oil.

10. Add garlic, bell pepper and broccoli.
11. Cook until crisp tender.
12. Season with the seasoning blend and pepper.
13. Put the tofu back and toss to mix.
14. Pour soy sauce mixture on top and transfer to serving bowls.
15. Garnish with the sesame seeds and serve on top of white rice.

Nutritional Value:

- Calories 400
- Protein 19 g
- Carbohydrates 45 g
- Fat 16 g
- Cholesterol 0 mg
- Sodium 584 mg
- Potassium 317 mg
- Phosphorus 177 mg
- Calcium 253 mg
- Fiber 2.7 g

# Broccoli Pancake

Preparation Time: 10 minutes
Cooking Time: 5 minutes
Servings: 4

Ingredients:

- 3 cups broccoli florets, diced
- 2 eggs, beaten
- 2 tablespoons all-purpose flour
- 1/2 cup onion, chopped
- 2 tablespoons olive oil

Method:

1. Boil broccoli in water for 5 minutes. Drain and set aside.
2. Mix egg and flour.
3. Add onion and broccoli to the mixture.
4. Pour oil in a pan over medium heat.
5. Cook the broccoli pancake until brown on both sides.

Nutritional Value:

- Calories 140
- Protein 6 g
- Carbohydrates 7 g
- Fat 10 g
- Cholesterol 106 mg
- Sodium 58 mg
- Potassium 276 mg
- Phosphorus 101 mg
- Calcium 50 mg
- Fiber 2.1 g

# Carrot Casserole

Preparation Time: 10 minutes
Cooking Time: 20 minutes
Serving: 8

Ingredients:

- 1 lb. carrots, sliced into rounds
- 12 low-sodium crackers
- 2 tablespoons butter
- 2 tablespoons onion, chopped
- 1/4 cup cheddar cheese, shredded

Method:

1. Preheat your oven to 350 degrees F.
2. Boil carrots in a pot of water until tender.
3. Drain the carrots and reserve ¼ cup liquid.
4. Mash carrots.
5. Add all the ingredients into the carrots except cheese.
6. Place the mashed carrots in a casserole dish.
7. Sprinkle cheese on top and bake in the oven for 15 minutes.

Nutritional Value:

- Calories 94
- Protein 2 g
- Carbohydrates 9 g
- Fat 6 g
- Cholesterol 13 mg
- Sodium 174 mg
- Potassium 153 mg
- Phosphorus 47 mg
- Calcium 66 mg
- Fiber 1.8 g

# Cauliflower Rice

Preparation Time: 10 minutes
Cooking Time: 10 minutes
Servings: 4

Ingredients:

- 1 head cauliflower, sliced into florets
- 1 tablespoon butter
- Black pepper to taste
- 1/4 teaspoon garlic powder
- 1/4 teaspoon herb seasoning blend

Method:

1. Put cauliflower florets in a food processor.
2. Pulse until consistency is similar to grain.
3. In a pan over medium heat, melt the butter and add the spices.
4. Toss cauliflower rice and cook for 10 minutes.
5. Fluff using a fork before serving.

Nutritional Value:

- Calories 47
- Protein 1 g
- Carbohydrates 4 g
- Fat 3 g
- Cholesterol 8 mg
- Sodium 43 mg
- Potassium 206 mg
- Phosphorus 31 mg
- Calcium 16 mg
- Fiber 1.4 g

# Eggplant Fries

Preparation Time: 10 minutes
Cooking Time: 5 minutes
Servings: 6

Ingredients:

- 2 eggs, beaten
- 1 cup almond milk
- 1 teaspoon hot sauce
- 3/4 cup cornstarch
- 3 teaspoons dry ranch seasoning mix
- 3/4 cup dry bread crumbs
- 1 eggplant, sliced into strips
- 1/2 cup oil

Method:

1. In a bowl, mix eggs, milk and hot sauce.
2. In a dish, mix cornstarch, seasoning and breadcrumbs.
3. Dip first the eggplant strips in the egg mixture.
4. Coat each strip with the cornstarch mixture.
5. Pour oil in a pan over medium heat.
6. Once hot, add the fries and cook for 3 minutes or until golden.

Nutritional Value:

- Calories 233
- Protein 5 g
- Carbohydrates 24 g
- Fat 13 g
- Cholesterol 48 mg
- Sodium 212 mg
- Potassium 215 mg
- Phosphorus 86 mg
- Calcium 70 mg
- Fiber 2.1 g

# Seasoned Green Beans

Preparation Time: 10 minutes
Cooking Time: 10 minutes
Servings: 4

Ingredients:

- 10 oz. green beans
- 4 teaspoons butter
- 1/4 cup onion, chopped
- 1/2 cup red bell pepper, chopped
- 1 teaspoon dried dill weed
- 1 teaspoon dried parsley
- 1/4 teaspoon black pepper

Method:

1. Boil green beans in a pot of water. Drain.
2. In a pan over medium heat, melt the butter and cook onion and bell pepper.
3. Season with dill and parsley.
4. Put the green beans back to the skillet.
5. Sprinkle pepper on top before serving.

Nutritional Value:

- Calories 67
- Protein 2 g
- Carbohydrates 8 g
- Fat 3 g
- Cholesterol 0 mg
- Sodium 55 mg
- Potassium 194 mg
- Phosphorus 32 mg
- Calcium 68 mg
- Fiber 4.0 g

# Grilled Squash

Preparation Time: 10 minutes
Cooking Time: 6 minutes
Servings: 8

Ingredients:

- 4 zucchinis, rinsed, drained and sliced
- 4 crookneck squash, rinsed, drained and sliced
- Cooking spray
- 1/4 teaspoon garlic powder
- 1/4 teaspoon black pepper

Method:

1. Arrange squash on a baking sheet.
2. Spray with oil.
3. Season with garlic powder and pepper.
4. Grill for 3 minutes per side or until tender but not too soft.

Nutritional Value:

- Calories 17
- Protein 1 g
- Carbohydrates 3 g
- Fat 0 g
- Cholesterol 0 mg
- Sodium 6 mg
- Potassium 262 mg
- Phosphorus 39 mg
- Calcium 16 mg
- Fiber 1.1 g

# Vegetable Medley

Preparation Time: 3 hours and 15 minutes
Cooking Time: 0 minutes
Servings: 12

Ingredients:

- 1 cup celery, chopped
- 2 cups mushrooms, sliced
- 1 cup green bell pepper, sliced
- 3 cups cauliflower florets, steamed and sliced
- 3 cups broccoli florets, steamed sliced
- 1 cup olive oil
- 1/2 cup onion, chopped
- 2 teaspoons dry mustard
- 1/2 cup sugar
- 1/2 cup vinegar
- 1 tablespoon poppy seeds

Method:

1. In a bowl, combine celery, mushrooms, bell pepper, cauliflower and broccoli.
2. In another bowl, mix the rest of the ingredients.
3. Marinate vegetables in the mixture for 3 hours in the refrigerator.
4. Remove from marinade before serving.

Nutritional Value:

- Calories 174
- Protein 2 g
- Carbohydrates 10 g
- Fat 14 g
- Cholesterol 0 mg
- Sodium 95 mg
- Potassium 250 mg
- Phosphorus 50 mg
- Calcium 33 mg
- Fiber 1.9 g

# Chapter 7: Snacks and Sides

## Mock Mashed Potatoes

Preparation Time: 10 minutes
Cooking Time: 10 minutes
Servings: 6

Ingredients:

- 6 cups cauliflower, chopped
- 4 oz. cream cheese
- 1 teaspoon garlic, crushed
- 1/2 teaspoon black pepper

Method:

1. Steam cauliflower until tender.
2. Drain and place in a blender.
3. Add the rest of the ingredients.
4. Pulse until smooth.

Nutritional Value:

- Calories 94
- Protein 3 g
- Carbohydrates 6 g
- Fat 7 g
- Cholesterol 19 mg
- Sodium 76 mg
- Potassium 198 mg
- Phosphorus 54 mg
- Calcium 22 mg
- Fiber 3.4 g

# Chicken in Lettuce Wraps

Preparation Time: 20 minutes
Cooking Time: 15 minutes
Servings: 4

**Ingredients:**

- 8 oz. chicken breast, cooked and cubed
- 2 scallions, chopped
- 2 teaspoons garlic, minced
- 2 tablespoons vegetable oil
- 1 tablespoon sesame oil
- 2 tablespoons rice vinegar
- 2 teaspoons hoisin sauce
- 1 teaspoon Chinese Five Spices seasoning
- 1/4 cup onion, chopped
- 1/4 cup fresh cilantro, chopped
- 1/4 cup mushroom, sliced
- 8 lettuce leaves

**Method:**

1. Mix all the ingredients in a pan over medium heat, except the onion, cilantro, mushroom and lettuce.
2. Cook for 15 minutes.
3. Remove the chicken and drain.
4. Place chicken cubes on top of each lettuce leaf.
5. Top with the onion, mushroom and cilantro.
6. Wrap and secure.

**Nutritional Value:**

- Calories 219
- Protein 17 g
- Carbohydrates 4 g
- Fat 15 g
- Cholesterol 51 mg
- Sodium 103 mg

- Potassium 225 mg
- Phosphorus 130 mg
- Calcium 25 mg
- Fiber 0.8 g

# Snack Mix

Preparation Time: 15 minutes
Cooking Time: 45 minutes
Servings: 12

Ingredients:

- Cooking spray
- 1 teaspoon cinnamon
- 2 tablespoons apple juice
- 1/2 cup sugar
- 1/4 cup egg whites, beaten
- 1 cup dried apples, diced
- 2 cups corn cereal
- 2 cups rice cereal
- 3 cups cinnamon cereal
- 1 cup dried cranberries, sliced
- 1 tablespoon sesame seeds

Method:

1. Preheat your oven to 300 degrees F.
2. Spray your baking pan with oil.
3. In a bowl, mix the egg whites, cinnamon, apple juice and sugar.
4. Mix the rest of the ingredients in another bowl and arrange on a single layer in the baking pan.
5. Pour egg mixture on top and stir to coat evenly.
6. Bake in the oven for 45 minutes.
7. Let cool before serving.

Nutritional Value:

- Calories 214
- Protein 3 g
- Carbohydrates 46 g
- Fat 2 g
- Cholesterol 0 mg
- Sodium 159 mg

- Potassium 118 mg
- Phosphorus 67 mg
- Calcium 84 mg
- Fiber 3.1 g

# Salmon Sandwich

Preparation Time: 10 minutes
Cooking Time: 12 minutes
Servings: 4

Ingredients:

- 2 tablespoons olive oil, divided
- 1 tablespoon lime juice
- 1/2 teaspoon lemon-pepper seasoning
- 4 salmon fillets
- 1/4 cup chipotle mayonnaise
- 4 slices sourdough bread
- 1 cup arugula
- 1/2 cup roasted red peppers, diced

Method:

1. Preheat your grill.
2. Coat salmon with half of the oil.
3. Grill salmon for 12 minutes.
4. In a bowl, mix the oil, lime juice and lemon pepper seasoning.
5. Toast the bread in the grill.
6. Spread mayo on the bread and arrange arugula and roasted red peppers.
7. Place salmon on top.

Nutritional Value:

- Calories 382
- Protein 26 g
- Carbohydrates 20 g
- Fat 22 g
- Cholesterol 68 mg
- Sodium 384 mg
- Potassium 640 mg
- Phosphorus 268 mg
- Calcium 45 mg
- Fiber 1.0 g

# Egg & Salsa Sandwich

Preparation Time: 5 minutes
Cooking Time: 5 minutes
Servings: 4

Ingredients:

- 2 tablespoons olive oil
- 6 eggs, beaten
- 8 slices white bread
- 4 teaspoons salsa

Method:

1. Pour oil in a pan over medium heat.
2. Cook scrambled eggs until firm.
3. Top white bread with salsa and eggs.
4. Place another slice on top.

Nutritional Value:

- Calories 327
- Protein 16 g
- Carbohydrates 32 g
- Fat 15 g
- Cholesterol 279 mg
- Sodium 318 mg
- Potassium 177 mg
- Phosphorus 272 mg
- Calcium 90 mg
- Fiber 6.0 g

# Beef & Dijon Sliders

Preparation Time: 15 minutes
Cooking Time: 15 minutes
Servings: 12

Ingredients:

- 1 1/2 lb. ground beef
- 1 tablespoon olive oil
- 1 onion, chopped
- 2 teaspoons Dijon mustard
- 12 dinner rolls, sliced in half

Method:

1. Create patties from the ground beef.
2. In a pan over medium heat, add oil and cook onion.
3. Stir in mustard.
4. Add beef patties on top.
5. Place the patties between the dinner rolls.

Nutritional Value:

- Calories 210
- Protein 14 g
- Carbohydrates 18 g
- Fat 9 g
- Cholesterol 52 mg
- Sodium 153 mg
- Potassium 193 mg
- Phosphorus 120 mg
- Calcium 13 mg
- Fiber 0.2 g

# Glazed Carrots

Preparation Time: 10 minutes
Cooking Time: 10 minutes
Servings: 4

Ingredients:

- 2 cups carrots
- 1/4 cup water
- 1 tablespoon sugar
- 1 teaspoon cornstarch
- 1/4 teaspoon ground ginger
- 1/4 cup apple juice
- 2 tablespoons butter

Method:

1. Boil carrots in a pot of water until tender.
2. While waiting, mix the rest of the ingredients.
3. Pour mixture into the pot.
4. Cook for 10 minutes.

Nutritional Value:

- Calories 101
- Protein 1 g
- Carbohydrates 14 g
- Fat 5 g
- Cholesterol 0 mg
- Sodium 170 mg
- Potassium 202 mg
- Phosphorus 26 mg
- Calcium 24 mg
- Fiber 2.7 g

# Cabbage with Mustard Sauce

Preparation Time: 10 minutes
Cooking Time: 8 minutes
Servings: 4

Ingredients:

- 1 tablespoon olive oil
- 3 tablespoons apple cider
- 2 tablespoons apple cider vinegar
- 1 tablespoon mustard
- 1/2 teaspoon caraway seeds
- 3 cups cabbage, shredded
- Cooking spray

Method:

1. Combine oil, cider, vinegar, mustard and seeds.
2. Spray oil on your pan.
3. Add cabbage and cook for 8 minutes, stirring frequently.
4. Pour the sauce over the cabbage.
5. Simmer for 5 minutes.

Nutritional Value:

- Calories 53
- Protein 1 g
- Carbohydrates 5 g
- Fat 3 g
- Cholesterol 0 mg
- Sodium 58 mg
- Potassium 154 mg
- Phosphorus 17 mg
- Calcium 27 mg
- Fiber 1.2 g

# Chapter 8: Poultry

## Crispy Lemon Chicken

Preparation Time: 10 minutes
Cooking Time: 20 minutes
Servings: 6

Ingredients:

- 6 chicken breast fillets, sliced into strips
- 1 teaspoon herb seasoning blend
- Black pepper to taste
- 1 egg
- 2 teaspoons water
- 1/2 cups all-purpose flour
- 2 tablespoons olive oil
- 1/2 cup lemon juice
- Parsley
- 4 cups steamed white rice

Method:

1. Season chicken with herb seasoning blend and black pepper.
2. In a bowl, mix the egg and water.
3. Dip chicken in the egg mixture and coat with flour.
4. Pour oil in a pan over medium heat.
5. Fry chicken until golden brown on both sides.
6. Sprinkle with lemon juice.
7. Garnish with parsley and serve with rice.

Nutritional Value:

- Calories 316
- Protein 22 g
- Carbohydrates 39 g
- Fat 8 g
- Cholesterol 82 mg

- Sodium 144 mg
- Potassium 234 mg
- Phosphorus 201 mg
- Calcium 28 mg
- Fiber 0.8 g

# Basil Chicken

Preparation Time: 15 minutes
Cooking Time: 25 minutes
Servings: 4

Ingredients:

- 4 chicken breast fillets
- 1/4 cup butter, melted
- 1/4 teaspoon garlic powder
- 1/4 cup fresh basil
- 1/4 teaspoon herb seasoning blend
- 1 tablespoon Parmesan cheese, grated

Method:

1. Preheat your oven to 325 degrees F.
2. Put the chicken breast fillet in a baking pan.
3. Combine butter, garlic powder, basil, herb seasoning and cheese.
4. Spread mixture over the chicken fillets, coating both sides.
5. Bake for 25 minutes.

Nutritional Value:

- Calories 252
- Protein 27 g
- Carbohydrates 0 g
- Fat 16 g
- Cholesterol 74 mg
- Sodium 231 mg
- Potassium 246 mg
- Phosphorus 210 mg
- Calcium 31 mg
- Fiber 0.1 g

# Turkey with Curry Glaze

Preparation Time: 10 minutes
Cooking Time: 30 minutes
Serving: 8

Ingredients:

- 3 lb. turkey breast fillet
- 1/4 cup butter, melted
- 1/4 cup honey
- 1 tablespoon mustard
- 2 teaspoons curry powder
- 1 teaspoon garlic powder

Method:

1. Add the turkey breast fillet on a roasting pan.
2. Bake at 350 degrees F in the oven for 1 hour.
3. While waiting, combine the rest of the ingredients in a bowl.
4. In the last 30 minutes of baking, brush the turkey breast with the mixture.
5. Let turkey sit for 15 minutes before slicing and serving.

Nutritional Value:

- Calories 275
- Protein 26 g
- Carbohydrates 9 g
- Fat 13 g
- Cholesterol 82 mg
- Sodium 122 mg
- Potassium 277 mg
- Phosphorus 193 mg
- Calcium 24 mg
- Fiber 0.2 g

# Rosemary Chicken with Veggies

Preparation Time: 20 minutes
Cooking Time: 45 minutes
Servings: 4

Ingredients:

- 1/2 onion, sliced into wedges
- 8 cloves garlic, crushed
- 1/2 bell pepper, sliced
- 1 carrots, sliced into rounds
- 2 zucchini, sliced into rounds
- 1 tablespoon olive oil
- 4 chicken breasts
- 1/4 teaspoon ground pepper
- 1 tablespoon dried rosemary

Method:

1. Preheat your oven to 375 degrees F.
2. Toss the onion, garlic, bell pepper, carrot and zucchini in a roasting pan.
3. Drizzle with oil.
4. Roast in the oven for 10 minutes.
5. While waiting, season chicken with pepper and rosemary.
6. Put the chicken on top of the vegetables.
7. Put them back in the oven.
8. Bake for 35 minutes.

Nutritional Value:

- Calories 215
- Protein 30 g
- Carbohydrates 8 g
- Fat 7 g
- Cholesterol 73 mg
- Sodium 107 mg
- Potassium 580 mg
- Phosphorus 250 mg

- Calcium 65 mg
- Fiber 3.0 g

# Sweet & Sour Chicken

Preparation Time: 15 minutes
Cooking Time: 20 minutes
Servings: 5

Ingredients:

- 1/4 cup apple cider vinegar
- 1 cup low-sodium chicken broth
- 1/4 cup brown sugar
- 1/2 teaspoon garlic, chopped
- 2 teaspoons low-sodium soy sauce
- 8 oz. canned pineapple chunks
- 1 lb. chicken breast, cubed
- 1 onion, diced
- 1 green bell pepper, sliced
- 1 cup celery, sliced
- 3 tablespoons cornstarch
- 1/4 cup water

Method:

1. Get the juice from the pineapple chunks.
2. Pour pineapple juice, vinegar, broth, sugar, garlic and soy sauce into a pan over low heat.
3. Add the chicken.
4. Cover the pan and simmer for 15 minutes.
5. Add the pineapple chunks and the vegetables.
6. Thicken the sauce using a mix of water and cornstarch.

Nutritional Value:

- Calories 310
- Protein 24 g
- Carbohydrates 47 g
- Fat 3 g
- Cholesterol 57 mg
- Sodium 270 mg

- Potassium 420 mg
- Phosphorus 211 mg
- Calcium 43 mg
- Fiber 1.6 g

# Turkey Meatloaf

Preparation Time: 15 minutes
Cooking Time: 1 hour
Servings: 6

Ingredients:

- 1 lb. ground turkey
- 3 ounces turkey sausage
- 1/2 cup dry breadcrumbs
- 2 eggs, beaten
- 1 tablespoon Worcestershire sauce
- 1 teaspoon Italian seasoning
- 1/4 cup fresh parsley, chopped
- 1/2 teaspoon black pepper

Method:

1. Preheat your oven to 350 degrees F.
2. Put all the ingredients in a bowl and mix.
3. Press mixture into a loaf pan.
4. Bake for 1 hour.

Nutritional Value:

- Calories 197
- Protein 20 g
- Carbohydrates 9 g
- Fat 9 g
- Cholesterol 85 mg
- Sodium 305 mg
- Potassium 314 mg
- Phosphorus 206 mg
- Calcium 49 mg
- Fiber 0.4 g

# Chicken Marsala

Preparation Time: 15 minutes
Cooking Time: 15 minutes
Servings: 4

Ingredients:

- 4 chicken breast fillets
- 1/2 cup all-purpose flour
- 2 tablespoons olive oil
- 1/2 cup shallots, chopped
- 2 cups fresh mushrooms, sliced
- 5 tablespoons fresh parsley, chopped
- 1 tablespoon butter mixed with 1 tablespoon olive oil
- 1/4 cup dry Marsala wine
- 1/4 teaspoon garlic powder
- 1/8 teaspoon black pepper

Method:

1. Coat both sides of chicken with flour.
2. Cook in hot oil in a pan over medium heat.
3. Cook until golden or for 5 minutes per side.
4. Put chicken on a platter and set aside.
5. Sauté mushrooms, parsley and shallots in olive oil butter blend for 3 minutes.
6. Add the rest of the ingredients.
7. Simmer for 2 minutes.
8. Pour sauce over chicken and serve with rice.

Nutritional Value:

- Calories 425
- Protein 32 g
- Carbohydrates 40 g
- Fat 15 g
- Cholesterol 70 mg
- Sodium 145 mg
- Potassium 480 mg

- Phosphorus 300 mg
- Calcium 46 mg
- Fiber 2.0 g

# Zesty Chicken

Preparation Time: 40 minutes
Cooking Time: 10 minutes
Servings: 2

Ingredients:

- 2 tablespoons olive oil
- 2 tablespoons balsamic vinegar
- 1/4 cup  green onion, chopped
- 1 teaspoon fresh oregano
- 1/2 teaspoon garlic powder
- 1/4 teaspoon black pepper
- 1/4 teaspoon paprika
- 8 ounces chicken breast fillets

Method:

1. Mix olive oil and vinegar.
2. Add green onion, herbs and seasonings.
3. Mix well.
4. Marinate chicken in the mixture for 30 minutes.
5. Cover and put inside the refrigerator.
6. Fry the chicken for 5 minutes per side.

Nutritional Value:

- Calories 280
- Protein 27 g
- Carbohydrates 4 g
- Fat 16 g
- Cholesterol 73 mg
- Sodium 68 mg
- Potassium 280 mg
- Phosphorus 205 mg
- Calcium 26 mg
- Fiber 0.3 g

# Chapter 9: Meat

## Beef & Broccoli

Preparation Time: 15 minutes
Cooking Time: 15 minutes
Servings: 4

Ingredients:

- 2 tablespoons peanut oil
- 2 cloves garlic, chopped
- 8 oz. sirloin beef, sliced into strips
- 4 cups broccoli, sliced into florets
- 1/4 cup low-sodium chicken broth
- 1 tablespoon cornstarch
- 2 tablespoons low-sodium soy sauce
- 2 cups cooked white rice

Method:

1. Heat oil in a pan over medium heat.
2. Cook the garlic for 30 seconds.
3. Add the broccoli and cook for 5 minutes.
4. Remove and set aside.
5. Add the beef and cook for 7 minutes.
6. Combine broth, soy sauce and cornstarch in a bowl.
7. Put the broccoli back to the pan.
8. Add the sauce and simmer until the sauce has thickened.
9. Serve with rice.

Nutritional Value:

- Calories 373
- Protein 18 g
- Carbohydrates 37 g
- Fat 17 g
- Cholesterol 42 mg
- Sodium 351 mg

- Potassium 555 mg
- Phosphorus 255 mg
- Calcium 62 mg
- Fiber 5.1 g

# Baked Pork Chops

Preparation Time: 15 minutes
Cooking Time: 40 minutes
Servings: 6

Ingredients:

- 1/2 cup all-purpose flour
- 1 egg, beaten
- 1/4 cup water
- 3/4 cup cornflake crumbs
- 6 pork chops
- 2 tablespoons butter
- 1 teaspoon paprika

Method:

1. Preheat your oven to 350 degrees F.
2. Put flour in a plate.
3. In a bowl, mix egg and water.
4. Add cornflakes in another bowl.
5. Coat each pork chop with flour, dip in the egg mixture and dredge with cornflakes.
6. Drizzle melted butter on top.
7. Sprinkle paprika on top of the butter.
8. Bake in the oven for 40 minutes.

Nutritional Value:

- Calories 282
- Protein 23 g
- Carbohydrates 25 g
- Fat 10 g
- Cholesterol 95 mg
- Sodium 263 mg
- Potassium 394 mg
- Phosphorus 203 mg
- Calcium 28 mg
- Fiber 1.4 g

# Balsamic Pork Chops

Preparation Time: 10 minutes
Cooking Time: 20 minutes
Servings: 4

Ingredients:

- 4 pork chops, trimmed
- 3 tablespoons balsamic vinegar
- 1/2 teaspoon dried thyme
- 1/2 teaspoon dried rosemary
- 1/4 teaspoon garlic powder
- 1/4 teaspoon black pepper
- 2 tablespoons vegetable oil
- 1 teaspoon unsalted butter
- 4 oz. mushrooms, sliced
- 1 onion, sliced

Method:

1. Coat pork chops with vinegar and season with herbs and spices.
2. Pour oil into a pan over medium heat.
3. Cook pork chops for 6 minutes.
4. Turn the pork chops and reduce heat.
5. Cover and cook for 10 minutes.
6. Transfer pork on a plate.
7. Add the butter, mushrooms and onions.
8. Cook for 2 minutes.
9. Pour the onion and mushroom with cooking liquid on top of the pork chops before serving.

Nutritional Value:

- Calories 285
- Protein 28 g
- Carbohydrates 5 g
- Fat 17 g
- Cholesterol 81 mg

- Sodium 79 mg
- Potassium 560 mg
- Phosphorus 274 mg
- Calcium 40 mg
- Fiber 0.7 g

# Braised Beef

Preparation Time: 20 minutes
Cooking Time: 1 hour and 30 minutes
Servings: 8

Ingredients:

- 2 lb. beef brisket, trimmed
- 2 teaspoons black pepper
- 2 tablespoons olive oil
- 1/2 onion, chopped
- 1 carrot, sliced
- 1 stalk celery, chopped
- 3 bay leaves, crumbled
- 1 tablespoon fresh parsley, chopped
- 2 cups low-sodium beef broth
- 3 cups water
- 2 tablespoons balsamic vinegar

Method:

1. Preheat your oven to 350 degrees F.
2. Season beef with black pepper.
3. Pour oil in a pot and brown the meat for 5 minutes per side.
4. Transfer meat to a plate and add onion, carrot and celery.
5. Cook for 4 minutes.
6. Add bay leaves and parsley.
7. Put the meat on top of the veggies.
8. Add the rest of the ingredients.
9. Cover and bring to a boil.
10. Transfer contents of pot to baking pan.
11. Bake in the oven for 1 hour.

Nutritional Value:

- Calories 230
- Protein 29 g
- Carbohydrates 4 g

- Fat 11 g
- Cholesterol 84 mg
- Sodium 178 mg
- Potassium 346 mg
- Phosphorus 193 mg
- Calcium 30 mg
- Fiber 0.8 g

# Herbed Pork Chops

Preparation Time: 15 minutes
Cooking Time: 15 minutes
Servings: 4

Ingredients:

- 4 pork chops
- 1 tablespoon fresh lime juice
- 1 tablespoon fresh cilantro, chopped
- 1/2 cup chives, chopped
- 2 green bell peppers, sliced into strips
- 1/8 teaspoon dried oregano leaves
- 1/4 teaspoon ground black pepper
- 1 tablespoon butter, melted
- 1/4 teaspoon ground cumin
- 1 tablespoon olive oil
- 1 lime

Method:

1. Coat pork chops with lime juice.
2. Season with cilantro.
3. Mix the oregano, pepper, butter and cumin.
4. Pour oil into a pan over medium heat.
5. Add the pork chops and cook for 4 minutes per side.
6. Add the oregano mixture and bell pepper.
7. Cook for 3 minutes.

Nutritional Value:

- Calories 265
- Protein 34 g
- Carbohydrates 24 g
- Fat 15 g
- Cholesterol 86 mg
- Sodium 70 mg
- Potassium 564 mg

- Phosphorus 240 mg
- Calcium 22 mg
- Fiber 1.0 g

# Dijon Pork Chops

Preparation Time: 15 minutes
Cooking Time: 15 minutes
Servings: 4

Ingredients:

- 4 pork loin chops
- 2 tablespoons all-purpose flour
- 1/4 cup shallots, chopped
- 2 teaspoons fresh ginger root, grated
- 1 tablespoon butter
- 1/2 cup low-sodium chicken broth
- 2 tablespoons dry sherry
- 2 teaspoons Dijon mustard
- 1 teaspoon mustard seed
- 1/8 teaspoon pepper
- Parsley

Method:

1. Coat both sides of pork chops with flour.
2. In a pan over medium heat, add the butter and cook pork chops until golden brown.
3. Place on a platter and keep warm.
4. Add sherry and broth to the skillet.
5. Bring to a boil.
6. Lower heat.
7. Add the shallots and ginger root.
8. Cook for 2 minutes.
9. Add the rest of the ingredients.
10. Pour the sauce over the pork chops before serving.

Nutritional Value:

- Calories 296
- Protein 27 g
- Carbohydrates 5 g

- Fat 17 g
- Cholesterol 78 mg
- Sodium 168 mg
- Potassium 438 mg
- Phosphorus 248 mg
- Calcium 34 mg
- Fiber 0.5 g

# Barbecue Beef

Preparation Time: 10 minutes
Cooking Time: 5 hours
Servings: 14

Ingredients:

- 3/4 cup brown sugar
- 12 oz. beer
- 8 oz. ketchup
- 4 lb. chuck roast
- 14 hamburger buns

Method:

1. Preheat your oven to 325 degrees F.
2. Combine beer, brown sugar and ketchup.
3. Add the roast in a baking pan.
4. Coat with the mixture.
5. Cover with foil.
6. Bake for 5 hours.
7. Slice meat or shred using a fork.
8. Serve on buns.

Nutritional Value:

- Calories 450
- Protein 33 g
- Carbohydrates 32 g
- Fat 21 g
- Cholesterol 92 mg
- Sodium 261 mg
- Potassium 357 mg
- Phosphorus 207 mg
- Calcium 85 mg
- Fiber 0.6 g

# Pork Souvlaki

Preparation Time: 1 hour
Cooking Time: 15 minutes
Servings: 6

Ingredients:

- 3 tablespoons lemon juice
- 1/4 cup olive oil
- 1/8 teaspoon black pepper
- 1 teaspoon dried oregano
- 1 lb. pork tenderloin, cubed
- 1 onion, sliced
- 2 cloves garlic, minced
- 1 bell green pepper, sliced

Method:

1. In a bowl, combine lemon juice, oil, pepper and oregano.
2. Marinate pork cubes in the mixture for 45 minutes inside the refrigerator.
3. Thread the pork, onion and bell pepper into skewers.
4. Grill for 15 minutes, turning halfway through.
5. Serve with rice or salad.

Nutritional Value:

- Calories 204
- Protein 18 g
- Carbohydrates 5 g
- Fat 13 g
- Cholesterol 53 mg
- Sodium 58 mg
- Potassium 336 mg
- Phosphorus 179 mg
- Calcium 17 mg
- Fiber 0 g

# Roasted Lamb

Preparation Time: 30 minutes
Cooking Time: 1 hour and 30 minutes
Servings: 10

Ingredients:

- 1/4 cup fresh rosemary leaves
- 2 tablespoons dried oregano
- 1 teaspoon black pepper
- 2 garlic cloves, minced
- 4 tablespoons butter, divided
- 1 leg of lamb, trimmed
- 1/4 cup fresh lemon juice
- 1 cup water

Method:

1. Preheat your oven to 325 degrees F.
2. In a bowl, combine the rosemary, oregano, pepper and garlic.
3. Stir in 2 tablespoons butter.
4. Create slits on both sides of the lamb using a sharp knife.
5. Stuff these slits with herb and butter mixture.
6. Coat the lamb with the remaining mixture.
7. Cover with foil and bake for 1 hour.
8. Uncover the lamb and bake for another 30 minutes.

Nutritional Value:

- Calories 318
- Protein 30 g
- Carbohydrates 0 g
- Fat 22 g
- Cholesterol 118 mg
- Sodium 114 mg
- Potassium 394 mg
- Phosphorus 228 mg
- Calcium 32 mg

- Fiber 0.5 g

# Italian Beef

Preparation Time: 30 minutes
Cooking Time: 5 hours and 45 minutes
Servings: 15

Ingredients:

- 3 lb. lean beef roast, trimmed
- 2 teaspoons oregano
- 2 teaspoons black pepper
- 1 teaspoon garlic powder
- 1 teaspoon red pepper, crushed
- 1 onion, sliced
- 1 green bell pepper, sliced
- 1 yellow bell pepper, sliced
- 1 red bell pepper, sliced
- 1/2 cup pepperoncini juice

Method:

1. Put all the ingredients except the bell peppers, onion and pepperoncini juice in a slow cooker.
2. Cook on high setting for 5 hours.
3. Shred beef and put it back to the pot.
4. Add the rest of the ingredients.
5. Cook on high setting for 45 minutes.

Nutritional Value:

- Calories 212
- Protein 25 g
- Carbohydrates 3 g
- Fat 11 g
- Cholesterol 84 mg
- Sodium 121 mg
- Potassium 280 mg
- Phosphorus 196 mg
- Calcium 21 mg
- Fiber 0.6 g

# Meat & Rice Balls

Preparation Time: 15 minutes
Cooking Time: 40 minutes
Servings: 4

Ingredients:

- 1 lb. lean ground beef
- 4 cups cooked white rice
- 1 egg
- 3/4 teaspoon herb seasoning blend
- 2 1/4 cups water

Method:

1. Mix the beef, rice and egg.
2. Roll and form 24 balls.
3. Cook the balls in a pan over medium heat.
4. Mix the herb seasoning and water.
5. Add the mixture to the pan.
6. Bring to a boil and then reduce heat and simmer covered for 30 minutes.

Nutritional Value:

- Calories 348
- Protein 24 g
- Carbohydrates 18 g
- Fat 20 g
- Cholesterol 131 mg
- Sodium 95 mg
- Potassium 350 mg
- Phosphorus 197 mg
- Calcium 21 mg
- Fiber 0.5 g

# Shish Kebabs

Preparation Time: 40 minutes
Cooking Time: 30 minutes
Servings: 6

Ingredients:

- 1/2 cup olive oil
- 1/2 cup white vinegar
- 1/4 teaspoon garlic powder
- 1/2 teaspoon oregano
- 1/4 teaspoon black pepper
- 1 1/2 pounds beef sirloin, cubed
- 2 onions, sliced
- 2 green bell peppers, sliced
- 1 red bell pepper, sliced

Method:

1. Combine oil, vinegar, garlic powder, oregano and pepper in a bowl.
2. Soak the beef cubes in the marinade for 30 minutes.
3. Thread beef cubes and vegetables into the skewers.
4. Grill for 30 minutes.

Nutritional Value:

- Calories 358
- Protein 26 g
- Carbohydrates 5 g
- Fat 26 g
- Cholesterol 80 mg
- Sodium 60 mg
- Potassium 458 mg
- Phosphorus 217 mg
- Calcium 25 mg
- Fiber 1.4 g

# Chapter 10: Desserts

## Vanilla Ice Cream

Preparation Time: 30 minutes
Cooking Time: 0 minutes
Servings: 8

Ingredients:

- 1 cup egg product
- 1/2 cup sugar
- 2 cups nondairy creamer
- 1 tablespoon vanilla extract
- Ice and rock salt

Method:

1. Beat egg product and sugar until mixed.
2. Add creamer and microwave the mixture for 1 minute.
3. Let it cool for 5 minutes.
4. Stir in the vanilla extract.
5. Pour the mixture into container of your ice cream machine.
6. Place ice and rock salt around the container.
7. Follow instructions for operating the ice cream machine.
8. Serve in ice cream cones or bowls.

Nutritional Value:

- Calories 159
- Protein 3 g
- Carbohydrates 22 g
- Fat 6 g
- Cholesterol 0 mg
- Sodium 64 mg
- Potassium 87 mg
- Phosphorus 36 mg
- Calcium 15 mg
- Fiber 0 g

# Apple Crisp

Preparation Time: 15 minutes
Cooking Time: 1 hour
Servings: 12

Ingredients:

- Cooking spray
- 5 apples, sliced
- 1 cup granulated sugar
- 1 cup all-purpose flour
- 1 teaspoon cinnamon
- 1 cup oatmeal
- 1 cup brown sugar
- 1/4 teaspoon baking soda
- 1/4 teaspoon baking powder
- 1/4 cup butter (unsalted)
- 1/4 cup shortening

Method:

1. Preheat your oven to 350 degrees F.
2. Spray baking pan with oil.
3. Combine all the ingredients and toss apple slices in the mixture.
4. Pour into the pan.
5. Bake for 1 hour.

Nutritional Value:

- Calories 308
- Protein 3 g
- Carbohydrates 54 g
- Fat 9 g
- Cholesterol 11 mg
- Sodium 45 mg
- Potassium 155 mg
- Phosphorus 56 mg
- Calcium 32 mg
- Fiber 2.0 g

# Baked Pineapple

Preparation Time: 10 minutes
Cooking Time: 30 minutes
Servings: 9

Ingredients:

- 20 oz. canned pineapple chunks
- 2 eggs
- 2 cups sugar
- 3 tablespoons tapioca
- 3 tablespoons butter (unsalted), cubed
- 1/2 teaspoon cinnamon

Method:

1. Preheat your oven to 350 degrees F.
2. Beat the eggs and combine with the pineapple chunks.
3. Add tapioca and sugar. Mix well.
4. Pour the mixture into a baking pan.
5. Place butter cubes on top and sprinkle with cinnamon.
6. Bake in the oven for 30 minutes.
7. You can serve it either warm or chilled.

Nutritional Value:

- Calories 270
- Protein 2 g
- Carbohydrates 54 g
- Fat 5 g
- Cholesterol 58 mg
- Sodium 50 mg
- Potassium 85 mg
- Phosphorus 26 mg
- Calcium 9 mg
- Fiber 0.6 g

# Creamy Vanilla

Preparation Time: 50 minutes
Cooking Time: 20 minutes
Servings: 15

Ingredients:

- 1 cup all-purpose flour
- 1 stick butter (unsalted), softened
- 1 cup granulated sugar
- 8 oz. cream cheese, softened
- 8 oz. whipped dessert topping, softened and divided
- 1 teaspoon vanilla extract
- 4 cartons vanilla pudding
- 1/2 cup coconut shreds

Method:

1. Preheat your oven to 350 degrees F.
2. Mix butter and flour.
3. Press mixture into a baking pan.
4. Bake for 20 minutes. Let cool for 10 minutes.
5. In a bowl, mix the sugar, cheese and dessert topping.
6. Spread this on top of the crust.
7. In another bowl, mix the vanilla extract and pudding.
8. Sprinkle coconut flakes on top.
9. Chill in the refrigerator for 30 minutes.

Nutritional Value:

- Calories 188
- Protein 2.1 g
- Carbohydrates 20 g
- Fat 11 g
- Cholesterol 33 mg
- Sodium 88 mg
- Potassium 29 mg
- Phosphorus 23 mg
- Calcium 15 mg
- Fiber 0.2 g

# Berries in Crepes

Preparation Time: 15 minutes
Cooking Time: 20 minutes
Servings: 4

Ingredients:

- 1/2 cup all-purpose flour
- 1/2 cup almond milk
- 2 egg whites, beaten
- 1 tablespoon vegetable oil
- Cooking spray
- 1/2 cup frozen berries (mix of strawberries, raspberries, blueberries), thawed and drained
- 1 tablespoon powdered sugar

Method:

1. In a bowl, mix the flour, almond milk, egg whites and oil.
2. Spray oil on your pan.
3. Turn the stove to medium heat.
4. Pour 1/4 cup of the flour mixture into the pan.
5. Let the batter spread by moving the pan in a circular motion.
6. Cook until golden.
7. Put the berries on top of the crepe.
8. Let it cook for another 2 minutes before folding the crepe in half.
9. Repeat for the rest of the batter.
10. Sprinkle powdered sugar on top before serving.

Nutritional Value:

- Calories 124
- Protein 5 g
- Carbohydrates 17 g
- Fat 4 g
- Cholesterol 0 mg
- Sodium 41 mg
- Potassium 123 mg

- Phosphorus 55 mg
- Calcium 47 mg
- Fiber 1.4 g

# Berry Cups

Preparation Time: 20 minutes
Cooking Time: 12 minutes
Servings: 12

Ingredients:

- 4 sheets phyllo pastry dough
- Cooking spray
- 1 cup blueberries
- 1 cup blackberries
- 1 cup raspberries
- 1 cup strawberries
- 3 cups frozen dessert topping

Method:

1. Preheat your oven to 400 degrees F.
2. Spray muffin pan with oil.
3. Layer the dough together but spray oil in between each sheet.
4. Cut the dough into smaller squares to fit into the pan to create dessert cups.
5. Bake these in the oven for 12 minutes.
6. Fill each cup with berries and dessert topping.

Nutritional Value:

- Calories 111
- Protein 2 g
- Carbohydrates 18 g
- Fat 4 g
- Cholesterol 0 mg
- Sodium 51 mg
- Potassium 83 mg
- Phosphorus 14 mg
- Calcium 19 mg
- Fiber 2.6 g

# Frozen Fruits

Preparation Time: 10 minutes
Cooking Time: 0 minute
Servings: 10

Ingredients:

- 1/4 cup cherries, chopped
- 8 oz. canned pineapple chunks, drained
- 8 oz. low-fat sour cream
- 1 tablespoon lemon juice
- 1 cup strawberries, sliced
- 1/2 cup sugar
- 3 cups dairy whipped topping

Method:

1. Put all the ingredients except the last one in a bowl.
2. Mix well and then fold in the topping.
3. Freeze the mixture for 2 hours.
4. Serve in bowls.

Nutritional Value:

- Calories 133
- Protein 1 g
- Carbohydrates 21 g
- Fat 5 g
- Cholesterol 21 mg
- Sodium 59 mg
- Potassium 99 mg
- Phosphorus 36 mg
- Calcium 47 mg
- Fiber 0.8 g

# Lemon Raspberry Mousse

Preparation Time: 4 hours and 30 minutes
Cooking Time: 1 minutes
Servings: 12

Ingredients:

- 48 vanilla wafers
- 1/4 cup granulated sugar
- 2 teaspoons lemon zest
- 8 oz. cream cheese
- 1 box lemon gelatin
- 3/4 cup boiling water
- 1 cup ice
- 4 scoops vanilla whey protein powder
- 8 ounces frozen dessert topping, thawed
- 1/4 cup raspberry preserves
- 1 cup raspberries, sliced

Method:

1. Cover your baking pan with cling wrap.
2. Arrange 16 vanilla wafers on the bottom part.
3. Beat the sugar, lemon zest and cream cheese in a mixer.
4. Transfer to a bowl.
5. In another bowl, pour in the gelatin powder and add hot water.
6. Stir until the powder has dissolved.
7. Add ice cubes.
8. Slowly add gelatin and protein powder to the cream cheese mixture.
9. Whisk the dessert topping and add to the bowl.
10. Pour half of the mixture on top of the wafers.
11. Put another layer of vanilla wafers.
12. In a pan, heat the raspberry preserves for 1 minute.
13. Spread on top of the vanilla wafers.
14. Add the remaining mixture on top.
15. Top with the remaining wafers.
16. Add raspberries on top of the last layer of wafers.

17. Refrigerate for 4 hours.

Nutritional Value:

- Calories 300
- Protein 12 g
- Carbohydrates 34 g
- Fat 13 g
- Cholesterol 42 mg
- Sodium 157 mg
- Potassium 92 mg
- Phosphorus 60 mg
- Calcium 44 mg
- Fiber 0.2 g

# Conclusion

Kidney disease is a serious health problem that you can take sitting down.
Not only should you take on a healthy kidney-friendly diet if you are at risk of or have already been diagnosed with kidney problem, you should also manage other medical conditions that can affect the kidneys, as well as maintain ideal weight.
Use the recipes mentioned in this book to give your kidneys a break.

Printed in Great Britain
by Amazon